A MOTTRAM MISCELLANY

A
Mottram
Miscellany

Rachel Young

The Larks Press

Published by
The Larks Press
Ordnance Farmhouse, Guist Bottom,
Dereham, Norfolk NR20 5PF

Fax/Tel. 01328 829207

October 1997

Printed by the Lanceni Press, Fakenham

British Library Cataloguing-in-Publication Data
A catalogue record for this book is available from the British
Library

Some of the letters in this book have previously been published in
'Portrait of an Unknown Victorian' by R.H. Mottram.
As far as is known none of the people mentioned in this book is
now living.

ISBN 0 948400 58 7

Preface

Some years ago I had the pleasure and privilege of working on some of the family papers of the Norwich writer, the late Ralph Hale Mottram. I am most grateful to his daughter, Sophia Hankinson, for introducing me to this delightfully varied collection. There are letters, printed papers, account books, diaries, travel journals, photographs, visiting cards, a lock of hair in an envelope, half a postcard on which is written 'Fredk Baker will vote for us W.W.'

Social history is now much more studied and much more highly esteemed than it was when I was young, but there are still unfortunately some people who think that real history consists of battles and politics and the dates of kings and queens and that social history is in some way trivial, but I think not. Social history is concerned with food, clothes, shelter, travel, work and above all with relationships between people which are the fundamentals of human life. What could be more essential? So whatever *they*, people in high places, say, I shall continue to enjoy my social history.

Rachel Young
Norwich 1997

Illustrations

The Mottram Papers 1730-1900
an introduction by Sophia Hankinson

These letters were accumulated by four generations of a Norwich family and are now at the Norfolk County Record Office. The generations were long ones - from the birth of James Nasmith Mottram senior in 1755 to the birth of his great-grandson, a century and a quarter. The only other unusual feature of the letters is their survival (unless the ordinariness of the lives they portray can be called extraordinary). In the hands of an expert social historian, however, they become part of a larger picture. To show how they fit together, a family tree is provided; the following notes are added for those afflicted with that most benign of contagions, genealogy.

Mottram is the name of two villages near Manchester, from which one family bearing that name had reached Lincolnshire, by way of Yorkshire, by the late 1500s. The first Thomas Mottram of whom we have a clear picture was Rector of Addlethorpe, a small village near Skegness, from 1580 to 1615, when he was buried in the fine old church there, as were some of his descendants. His will shows him to have been a man of substance, and that of his great-grandson Samuel (of 1710) starts with three pages of bequests to the church and the poor of the village; the cottages he endowed still stand close by.

John Mottram, grandson of Thomas, moved to Norwich, becoming a freeman of the city as a weaver in 1655. There is a tradition (in Addlethorpe) that the Mottrams 'were Quakers', and (in the family) that John came east with the Independent minister Martyn Finch. A John Mottram was at St Lawrence, which seems to have been a tolerant church, in the difficult 1680s and 90s. He may have worshipped previously at St Stephen's, leaving when Dr John Collings resigned there in 1662; the same John was one of two original trustees of the land on which the Presbyterian meeting-house, predecessor of the Octagon Chapel, was built for Collings in Colegate in 1689.

The Addlethorpe 'cozens' kept in touch, as their wills show; they seem to have been well-to-do and affectionate to their daughters as well as sons. Samuel left money to Elizabeth, who was 'in my family', and to

James Nasmith Senoir and Mary Crabb, his wife.

Lydia, about 1710. They were daughters of his cousin Deborah, John's sister, who had married Sir Thomas Churchman of Norwich - would that we had *her* letters! - but that is another story.

John's surviving son was last heard of in the East Indies, and it was Samuel's brother Thomas (the fourth, c. 1660-1729, 'of Trowse'), who came to Norwich as apprentice to his uncle John; he later inherited John's 'havills stays and loom which he used to weave in and all his old mill harns and trundle except the silk trundle'. Some of his children were baptised both at St Lawrence and at the Presbyterian meeting; his sons Thomas (the fifth, born 1710, freeman as a woolcomber 1731) and Samuel (1712-85, also a weaver) begin to appear regularly in Norwich documents. Mottram baptisms, marriages and burials are recorded in the registers of the adjoining parishes of St Saviour, St George's Colegate, St Michael at Plea and St Andrew's, and more than one family wedding was held in St Luke's Chapel of the Cathedral.

Thomas V was landlord of the King's Arms in St Michael at Plea till 1786, when he moved to London. He married Jane Nasmith, daughter of the carrier, and author of the earliest letter in this selection. His brother Samuel, who had no children, was treasurer of the Octagon Chapel building fund, to which he and Thomas were contributors, along with Nasmiths, Marshes, Smiths and Columbines, with whom they were now connected by marriage.

James Nasmith Mottram senior, son of Thomas V, was the first of four generations to work in Gurney's Bank and live 'over the shop' from 1779. He had been at school with Bartlett Gurney who founded the bank (originally in Magdalen Street, soon moving to the present site of Barclays Bank Plain opposite the King's Arms). His son James Nasmith Mottram junior lived in 20 Castle Meadow until 1850 when he moved into Gurney's Bank House with his family. Another James (1834-1915) continued a connection which ended only when his son, Ralph, left the bank to become a full time writer in 1924.

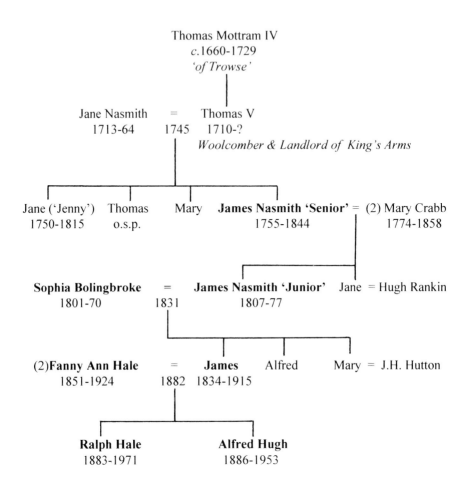

Part of the Mottram family tree

A Mottram Miscellany

-❀-

Letters are a unique source for the social historian. Usually written with no thought of publication, personal, informal, sometimes indiscreet, they have a vitality and immediacy lacking in more formal and official communications. The more obscure the writer, the more valuable the letter, for social history is concerned with everyday lives of ordinary people, most of whom have disappeared leaving no trace behind.

Some of the letters from the Mottram papers show how attitudes to marriage and married life have changed over two centuries. In this letter to her cousin Polly, Jane Nasmith, who later became Mrs Thomas Mottram, expresses an attitude to marriage very usual in her time. The letter is now slightly damaged but the sense is clear.

Norw. Janr 13th 173 -

[Dear] Polly,

I was a Stranger to yor long stay at Bury & began to suspect from that absence, & more agreeable Objects had erac'd me from yor Memory; but you [can] imagine, than it's possible for me to express, the infinite pleasure your Letter gave me, [especially] that part where I find myself so happy, as sometimes to have a place in yor Thoughts [I am] pleas'd with yor management in that troublesome Affair, you had to act in...., & think yor Prudence, & good Nature, made it a much easier Task than I [feared it might] have been: but my dear Polly I'm impatient to know the Success you met with [among the] widowers; I'm very certain the Conquest you wrote me word of, is not the only one [you made in] Sudbury; pray in yor next give me a particular Account (without the least reserve) [of the] Man that stood fairest in yor Esteem.

[There is Nothing] but Weddings talk'd of here. Mr Harvey was Yesterday married to Miss ... [and there] are a great many more wch are very near concluded. they say Mr Press pays [attention to] Miss Flatman, & declares himself to be worth ten thousand pound. I've not yet [heard the] Reception he met with, but that Sum has captivating Charms, & generally pleads with too [much eloquence] to be refused by the Ladies, it answers all their Objections, & indeed no Argument [is offered]. I mention'd the Match because I thought you hd some knowledge of Miss Flatman.

[I should have] begun wth my Indisposition to have apologis'd for my silence, I've had a violent [disorder in] my Eyes wch made me incapable of writing, & they are now so weak that I dare not [do much with] them for fear of the Consequences, when they are better you shall have a longer [letter].

[Mrs] Nasmith desir'd me to give you an Invitation to Norw. in wch we all join [& most earnestly] wish you'll accept of it. I've a thousand things to say which I dare not [put in writing] but refer them till we have the pleasure of meeting. But my services to Mr Crompton. Its not too late to give you the Compliments of the Season & may you enjoy return of many happy new Years is the sincere wish of

> Yor obligd Friend
> & humble Servt
> J.N.   In vast haste

Jane Nasmith's father was a carrier; his heavy horse-drawn wagons plied between Norwich and Birmingham, taking several days on the journey. Polly presumably came from a similar background. If these young women had been the daughters of aristocrats, their marriages would have been arranged for them, though they would have had to give their formal consent, both before the engagement and during the wedding ceremony. As it was, Polly was doing her own husband-hunting among the widowers of Bury St Edmunds, though, having attracted a suitor, he would be expected to approach her father and convince him that this would be a desirable alliance. A widower who was comfortably off, used to married life, with his own home and a settled occupation, might well be considered by both father and daughter as a better bet than a young man with his way to make. The widower, for his part, would probably be anxious to marry again, particularly if he had young children. If he was some years older than his second wife, this would not be considered a disadvantage.

The attitude to marriage expressed in Jane Nasmith's letter may seem to us cynical and mercenary. To most of her contemporaries, however, it would appear eminently sensible. Most people thought, as their predecessors had done for ages past, that romantic passion was not a good basis for marriage. Such feelings, they argued, did not last and could cause people to do foolish things, like marrying someone who had no money. Girls like Jane and Polly were looking for, and expected to look for, a marriage that would give them economic security, enhanced status (a married woman took precedence over an unmarried one), their own home, companionship and children. In return the wife would expect to manage the house and look after the children, more often than not she would also help her husband in his business.

A letter from Jane's sister, Mary Nasmith, dated Nov 19, 1742, shows that marriage to a complaisant widower might well be preferable to the life of an unmarried daughter at home.

Dearest Frind,

Your agreeable letters of the 15th Oct lay now on the table & to make ashmed at my silence, believe me its not Negligence or forgetfullness of my Dear Polly that her letter is not Answered, but several Accidents & some Business that has prevented. My Mother has been Ill three weeks, confin'd to the Chamber the greatest Part of the Time, & so tedious the whole Family was scarcely Sufficient to attend her, she is better & in the Parlour again. at the same Time our Cook Maid was taken with a Violent Fever, we were obliged to send her to her Mother's, & the Town is so full of the small Pox, that what with nursing the sick, & those that were fresh up of them, we can't get us a Servant in her Place, & to add to our Troubles the greatest Washing we have had for twelve Months, have been in hand, we finished Ironing last Night according to Custom have catch'd a Violent Cold having Settled on my Stomach & with it Became greatly opprest, must beg the Favour of you to send me the Receipt for the Astma you gave me when at Walpole, I left it in Miss Biddy's work Basket. My service to Mr Crompton. I sincerely Condole with him for the loss of his Boy, hope the Misfortune is not so great but in Time it may be retrieved, have sent him the Pamphlet on Practice, hope he'll excuse its not coming before, for could not procure one sooner, what the box contain besides beg your acceptance, the Cap from my Mother, Mr Frost's Sermons (I am sorry there is but one against the folly of Drunknenness Sister Marsh can fine no more, desire Biddy & you would not Coif for it) a Piece of Satten for Shoes & half a Dozin Oat Cakes which our Coach Man made me a Present of one Wednesday, my Cold makes me very low Spirited, I can't write you one Piece of News will you forgive the Dullness of your Frinde I hope to amend & give a better Account of Self in my next. Our Family joyne with me in due Compliments to Mr & Mrs Crompton your Self & Miss Biddy, my Service to Mrs Stroger Mr & Mrs Colson & all Frinds that ask for Dear Polly

Your Sincere Frind & obliged
humble Servant
M Nasmith

Norw. Nov 19 1742.

4

The kind of marriage that Jane and Mary sought has been described as a business partnership with an agreeable companion; it was usually very stable. It was what careful business and professional men and skilled artisans wanted for their children and what the children usually wanted for themselves. For instance Thomas Turner, a Sussex shopkeeper (1729-1793) stated in his diary his belief that one should not wed to gratify an inordinate passion, either for romance or for wealth. The woman whom he finally married on April 14th 1760 was thirty years old (he was thirty-six), he described her as clean and neatly dressed, though not pretty, no scholar but pleasant and sensible. She had been in good service, so would be able to run his house efficiently; she had probably accumulated some savings; she might inherit some money. So far as we know this was a satisfactory marriage, they remained together until his death, twenty-eight years later.

Similarly John Secker, a Norfolk man, after having worked as a sailor for twenty-five years, left the sea when he was nearly forty and needed to find some other means of livelihood. So, as he wrote in his journal, 'I made choice of a woman about my own age. She was newly got into a shop'. Having married Phoebe Ransome and her shop in March 1756, John spent the rest of his life as a successful and much respected grocer, first in Ashill, Norfolk, and then in Holt. But he would not have married Phoebe, however many shops she had inherited, if she had not been a Quaker like himself. In these 'prudent' marriages, if they were to be regarded with approval, there were always other considerations besides purely economic ones.

But by the time Thomas Turner and John Secker married, such unions were increasingly criticized. Loveless, mercenary marriages were condemned by preachers, mocked by dramatists. By the end of the eighteenth century many people felt that the partners in a marriage, however suitable the match in other ways, must also be and remain passionately in love with each other and should continue to express their mutual devotion throughout their married life. As did Sophia Bolingbroke - Ralph Mottram's grandmother -

Sophia Bolingbroke and her husband
James Nasmith Mottram Junior- married 1831

who married James Nasmith Mottram junior in 1831. Before her marriage, she wrote frequently to James expressing her love, admiration, and respect for him. She went on doing this after her marriage, whenever she and her husband were separated. When she took the children to Yarmouth, she wrote almost daily to her husband in Norwich, telling him how much she loved him, how much she missed him, how she could not enjoy the holiday without him, how life did not seem quite real if he was not with her. On July 22nd 1832 she wrote 'I cannot tell you how much I have missed you and wished for you'. His love and approbation, she wrote, were dearer to her than anything else, 'life without them would be worthless to me'. Today, this might seem somewhat exaggerated, but in the 1830s, educated people were expected to have strong feelings and to express them. One has only to think of Queen Victoria's letters with all those exclamation marks and underlinings. If an MP, at a suitable moment, burst into tears in the House of Commons, this was quite acceptable as evidence of the Honourable Member's sensitivity. If it happened now, everyone would be acutely embarrassed. Our views as to how and when to express emotion have changed. But there continued to be an economic element in a 'suitable' marriage. The bridegroom should make provision for his wife if she outlived him; the bride was expected to bring some money with her, as well as household goods, particularly bedlinen. On April 12 1827, James Nasmith Mottram senior noted in his accounts 'To Hugh Rankin on his marriage to my daughter Jane Mottram £100'.

Soon after her marriage on April 23 1833, Sophia wrote a letter to be given to her husband when she died. She added to this from time to time; the last entry is dated September 24, 1848. In this pious and effusive serial letter she reiterates her conviction that she would die first. Every time she was pregnant, she expected to die in childbirth. Her fear of early death is understandable. She was one of thirteen children, eight of whom were dead before she married at the age of 31 and it was only too common for women to die giving birth; often the baby died too. Sophia, however, was

James Nasmith Mottram Junior at the time of his wife's death in 1870

fortunate: she only had three children, all of whom survived to grow up and have children of their own. She herself lived to be sixty-nine though, as she expected, her husband survived her. The Mottrams were perhaps a more robust stock than the Bolingbrokes. Even so, Sophia's husband, James Nasmith Mottram, was the third son to be given this name; both his older brothers died as infants, one aged five weeks and the other nine months.

Ralph Mottram's mother, born Fanny Ann Hale, had a very different attitude to married life. She was happy with her husband, devoted to her two sons, determined to do her best for her three stepdaughters, James' children by his first wife. But from the first Fanny took it for granted that she should have interests and activities outside the home. When she married James Mottram on June 20 1882, she had for years earned her living as a music teacher. She continued to teach and to add to her professional qualifications. She joined the Brontë Society and the Dante Circle; she attended University Extension lectures. She was an active member of the Women's Liberal Association. In later years she worked on the Education and Child Welfare Committee of the City Council as a co-opted member. Her diary for 1899 shows her attending lectures on Dante and meetings of the Camera Club but also visiting in Pottergate on behalf of the Norwich Sick Poor Society and every Wednesday attending a sewing circle which made clothes for the poor.

As she had ample domestic help (four maids living in, plus a weekly washerwoman and a part-time bootboy), she had more free time than most professional women with children enjoy today. She did not waste it. Letters in the collection show that she often left her family in order to visit friends and relatives in, amongst other places, Manchester, Leicester, Chesterfield (she sent Ralph, then nearly eight, a drawing of the crooked spire of the parish church), London and the Isle of Man. Educated in France, she loved to travel on the Continent. At the beginning of 1893 she spent six weeks exploring the Riviera, leaving the day before her younger son's seventh birthday. A letter from her friend Maria

Clarke, who established the Surrey House School, where Fanny had pupils, shows how the boys reacted.

The postscript is
done entirely by
himself   Surrey House
27.1.93   Norwich
Friday   6.45 p.m.

Dearest,
        Ralph came just before the work cl[ass] was over & after a salutation went into the dining room & [took] a Punch - then we came up to my room together to do the lessons - but a good cry opened the proceedings but with the tears still copiously flowing he wanted to attack his lessons - but we dried our tears first - & as he was cold in hands etc - we again went down - Amelia saw our troubles & brought us a private tea into the dining room - but meantime the lessons, quite easy for him were done - & one being Geography and involving a map - started a pleasant interest - then came tea a lovely egg - & some French toast, were highly praised & enjoyed - & his appreciation of kindness - (like his Mother's) & pleasant chat made it quite a happy time, but before this, when Mary came for Hugh (who went off as bright as buttons) I wrote a note to Kitty saying that as I was anxious to see how he was in the morning, I had decided to keep him, tonight - this decision had cheered him a good deal. Now since tea we've stretched my bed - with 3 chairs a stool - an extra little featherbed etc, he helping - & now is gone cheerfully to read his Punch while I write this; I feel convinced that the worst is now passed for him & that except the little troubles of each day at school, which we must try to meet as they come, he will soon be as usual. Meanwhile dearest - how I would like to comfort you. I can only say be strong, my brave earnest precious - Trust the good ruler - we

10

more & more believe in - although all the Problems become more & more complex with new knowledge & experience. And for the month before you - there will be new <u>power</u> to be gained thru' the New Experiences, that may be of value some day, & there will be some beauty & love in it, & <u>wonder</u> at Nature's beauties, & who knows what beside? and the rest we must leave, hoping to be restored to each other & to work

Adieu my most Precious one

yrs Maria Clarke.

[Postscript in Ralph's handwriting]

Dear Mother,
    I have got on very well. I know my lessons very well, and am going to sleep at Surrey House. I shall write to you soon.

Ralph

In the summer of 1897 she and Maria Clarke spent three weeks abroad. On August 23rd they were in Switzerland, where they crossed a glacier, roped together, a guide cutting steps for them in the ice. It was raining and very slippery; their long, voluminous skirts, heavy and wet, must have added to their problems. But Fanny wrote in her diary that she felt 'richer by an unique experience which, with all its terrors, we would not on any account have missed'. She was forty-six, but with her appetite for trying new things undiminished. Later in the holiday she and her friend went sight-seeing in Cologne, even though it was pouring with rain. At home, she explored the countryside on her bicycle. Ralph said that she was the first lady to ride a cycle in Norwich, wearing a specially designed skirt attached to her ankles so that she did not show more leg than was proper for the wife of a bank

Fanny Ann Mottram and her husband James Mottram in 1910.
They were married in 1882

manager. Her husband did not care for 'abroad'. In the winter of 1887, however, he was persuaded to go on holiday to the Continent. He did not enjoy it and was soon very homesick. From Italy on November 29th he wrote that he missed England 'and all English ways'. By December he was longing for home. His letters to his wife in the Spring of 1888, when he was walking in the North Riding, were much more cheerful. One, from Helmsley, ends 'I have come in tonight with primroses in my coat'.

In her day, Fanny would have been described as an example of the New Woman. She campaigned for votes for women, better education and career opportunities for girls, better conditions for working women. She raised the wages of her maids and rearranged their work so that they could have regular time off. She insisted that her stepdaughters, Kitty and Helen, should go abroad, learn languages, acquire qualifications and equip themselves to work as teachers (the other daughter, Ethel, was too delicate for this). Amongst the papers is a diary kept by Helen when, at the age of twenty, she was at school at Sèvres. She worked for examinations alternated with educational trips to Paris to visit the Louvre, the opera, the theatre - she saw Sarah Bernhardt play 'Joan of Arc' and was 'a little disappointed' - and various 'sights' including the catacombs which she found 'strange but not very interesting'. She became a teacher at Darlington, where she took a further examination in French and German, attaining 1st class Honours with Distinction.

James was fifty when he remarried - eighteen years older than his new wife - and no doubt somewhat set in his ways. Fanny loved cycling but James never learnt; Fanny was using a typewriter by March 1885, when she sent Ralph a letter she had typed; it is unlikely that James ever did. Nevertheless, he was just as keen on self-improvement as she was and determined to use his limited leisure to good purpose. His interests, however, were different. He acquired a microscope, helped to form a small group of enthusiasts who met in each other's houses, did his best to interest others. On Sunday, May 8th 1887, he wrote to his wife that Thomas Southwell

Gurney's Bank House in 1786 - James Mottram set up his telescope on the roof

- a distinguished amateur naturalist - 'is coming to supper to see microscope, also Mrs Freeman and her visitor coming to tea for the same purpose'. In the 1880s he became fascinated by astronomy. He bought two large telescopes and had them mounted on a platform on the roof of the Bank House. His aunt, Eliza Johnson, wrote to him on November 5th 1882 'Have you seen the comet? To be sure you have - You would sit up all night rather than not see it! I suppose your wife does not ascend the ladder and sit shivering at the top of the house! or has she caught your enthusiasm?'

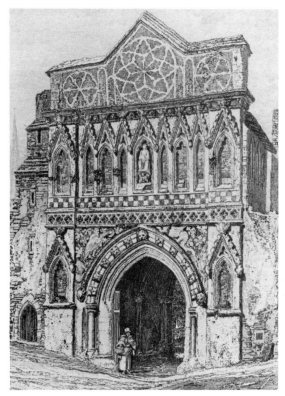

John Sell Cotman's etching of the Ethelbert Gate of Norwich Cathedral in 1817 - Fanny and James attended choir rehearsals in the room above the gateway

James and Fanny shared a passion for music. They first met as members of the Gate House Choral Society, which used the room above the Ethelbert Gate of Norwich Cathedral for rehearsals. On December 7th 1881 James wrote rather coyly to the conductor of this Society, inviting him to guess 'which of the single ladies of the Gate House is most suited to be my wife'.

Fanny played the piano and sang; James played the cornet, trumpet, double bass and cello. He sang in the chorus at the Triennial Festival for nearly fifty years and became involved in the organisation of the Festival. Distinguished participants were offered hospitality at the Bank House. Sir Alexander Mackensie, who

15

eventually became Director of the Royal Academy of Music, stayed with the Mottrams for the Triennial Festival of 1884 and became a friend. There are letters from him in this collection. On August 20th 1897 he wrote:

Fern Nook
Ilkley
Yorks
Aug 20 [1897?]

My Dear Mottram,

My daughter, who is staying with us here for a few days, tells me that you paid us a visit and found an empty house. For the which I am very sorry, as I would have liked very much to have seen you. As a matter of fact, I was so tired after a heavy year's work, that I left the day after my affairs at the R.A.M. were wound up; made a quick bolt of it to this delightful place <u>on the moars</u> (we are literally in a little house on the hills, not in the town) All the more reason, as I had to spend a dreadful week in Wales (Newport) at an Eisteddford (probably my very last) where they disputed our judgements and generally behaved like raving maniacs. Since then, however I have pretty well recovered from my fatigues and am doing a little bit of work for the Hayworth Theatre, just to keep my hand in. But we are out a great deal and take every advantage of the fine air ..

I hope you will come to town soon again and be sure to let me know so that you can lunch or dine with us and let us have our crack, as the Scotch say ...

Elgar came to the Festival in 1899 for the first performance of his song cycle 'Sea Pictures', sung by Clara Butt. He stayed a week with the Mottrams and proved a somewhat troublesome visitor. He was so nervous on the night before the performance that his wife, alarmed, woke her host. On October 19th, Elgar wrote:

at 3 Tedworth Square
Chelsea S.W.
Oct 19 1899

My dear Mr Mottram:
After all our exciting times comes a quiet day
and I must wish to send you a little line to thank you for all
your kindness to us in Norwich. I hope you have settled
down to, perhaps, a comparatively unmusical time after the
Homeric doings of the Festival week. I don't think I can ever
be sufficiently apologetic for my miserable health during
those days & the consequent trouble to Mrs Mottram & your
household. I only hope I am quite forgiven - King Olaf at
Sheffield was a great triumph but the orchestra was not much
good & made us long for the superb orchestra at Norwich.
We are remaining here (in dense fog) until Tuesday
when we return to our quiet woods & hills and - it may be
- to write some more music.
With our united kindest regards to Mrs Mottram &
yourself believe me
Sincerely yours
Edward Elgar

I hope Ralph is all right again after his hard week's work?

Both Mr and Mrs James Mottram were active members of the
Unitarian Octagon Chapel in Colegate, Norwich. James' forbears
had for generations played a prominent part in the affairs of this
chapel and its predecessor. There was a strong musical tradition at
the Octagon which would appeal to both James and Fanny - James
played the trumpet in the band of the Chapel's Friendly Society.
The Octagon was the first place of worship in Norwich, outside the
Cathedral, to have a trained choir, with some paid singers. This
could cause problems, as can be seen from the letter sent to James'
father on April 15th 1847 by Henry Martineau about the unfor-

The Norwich Octagon Chapel
Exterior drawn by James Sillett. Interior drawn by Maria Clarke.

18

tunate situation which had arisen when the minister, Mr Crompton, had chosen a hymn which the choir, very small that day, had sung badly. The organist, Mr Barker, was angry, did not play a voluntary, and complained loudly about the minister's choice of hymn and the fact that the girls from the Octagon Girls' School were sitting in the Singers' Gallery. 'I at once removed them' wrote Henry Martineau 'not choosing them to hear such a display of temper in reference to their minister'. He added:

> I was not in Norwich when Mr Crompton preached on the subject of Congregational Singing, but I have heard from those on whose report I can fully rely, his object was to encourage a devotional spirit in this part of the service; it is to be regretted therefore it should be made a subject of disagreement on all sides. It is very easy to find fault with the present singing or to compare it with what it was in the days of Mr Ed. Taylor etc. etc., but with such amateurs as then were willing & able to assist & who took an interest in having the music properly performed, the duty of an organist was very different to what it now is, when it seems a chance whether the Singers go to the Singing Gallery or any other part of the Chapel.

He went on to say that in the past members of the congregation had subscribed to hire professional singers but that money for this was no longer collected. He had offered to supply some trebles from among the school children. His letter continues:

> That plan has failed & I think the next best thing to be done is to get Subscriptions for four good Voices Treble, Tenor, Counter-tenor & Bass, approved by Mr Barker & that he having the authority his office gives should hold a weekly practise & fix the tunes before the Sunday. Without he feels secure of the regular attendance of some singers on whom he can rely no efficient practise will be kept up, & I do not see

19

that having four singers who understand what they have to do, need prevent many of the present ones joining, & they would be an assistance to our less experienced ones who require the support more practised voices would give. I feel sure no plan can succeed that is not under the superintendance of the organist. If admitting strangers be objected to, as making too much of a musical display which need not be the case (as I only wish to have the singing well done, if done at all) or if it is thought they will only attend to the music & not to the Service, I fear I must say from experience, there is likely to be quite as much attention as from many of our own people whose conduct in the Singing Gallery has often been anything but what it should be. I am quite ready to admit the assistance of such inexperienced singers as the Girls was of much less use lately, than when Mr B. furnished the tunes, then either Miss Athow or I made a point of hearing them every Saturday, & had that plan been continued since Xmas I feel sure they would have been of use. I should be very sorry to lose Mr Barker, & shall be very glad to find you can with him consider some plan, that he may think a good one & I think when we see how earnestly Mr Crompton performs his part of the service, the least that can be done is for the Congregation to do their utmost to unite in assisting in their part in a right spirit, & for the Deacons to insist on the punctual discharge of the organist's duties, on his not using such language as we heard, & at the same time not to allow him to be blamed for a failure which is no fault of his. I have written more than I intended, & hoping you will excuse the length of my note & that your deliberations may end in Harmony remain

Yrs very truly

H Martineau

Bracondale
Ap 15th 1847

20

A month later, Henry was threatening to resign from the choir unless it improved.

[Henry Martinueau was a brother of the writer Harriet Martineau. Edward Taylor had played an important part in the musical life of the chapel and written many hymns for it, before he moved to London where, in 1837, he became Gresham Professor of Music at the University of London.]

At the Octagon, as elsewhere, Fanny had her own activities. She helped to start a club for girls, anxious, as always, to increase opportunities for women. By the end of the 19th century there was an urgent need for this. Millions of young single men had left England to work or to settle abroad. Few returned to wed, so more and more English women remained unmarried. There was, in the dismissive phrase of the time, a problem of 'surplus women'. A working class girl could usually, as long as her strength held out, support herself by factory work or domestic service. It was now essential that there should be more paid occupations open to middle class women and that girls should be educated in such a way that they could, if necessary, earn their own living.

Among the young men who left England to seek their fortune overseas were two of Fanny Mottram's uncles, Frederick and Henry Hale. There are letters from both of them in this collection. The Hales were a middle class family who by the end of 1833 were impoverished and in debt. A letter from Frederick, then sixteen, to his eldest brother Alfred shows that the rest of the family, who had moved to London, were struggling to keep going.

Mr Alfred Hale   Steeple Ashton   Wilts
Post Paid   Retreat, Vauxhall
                                                   Novr 17th 1833
  Dear Alfred
       Through our old friend Mr New I have taken the

opportunity of writing to you. I still go on with my French, which I should not be able to do if it was not for his kindness. I am with Mr Penn as yet, but Mr New has been trying very much to get me a better situation. I have asked Mr Penn to give me something a week, but he said that Henry & Christopher had been educated for nothing, therefore he did not propose anything but said he would give me a present at Christmas.

Henry has been at a Stay-makers as Errand Boy, where, he had his board and 3d a week. He is now at a Tailors in the same way, he boards with us, and they give him 8/- a week. Father thought the Stay-makers very bad for him for the people were always drinking.

Uncle put me in posses[s]ion of the Furniture Chattels &c at the Retreat House, Mr Barber who resided there, not being able to pay the Rent, £55 for half year. He took the house for 28 years he tried to sell the Lease but could not, there not being scarcely a bidder. Barber went to the Sale, which was very foolish knowing he was in debt, everywhere. However he was seen & arrested for a debt of £37 & flung into Whitecross prison no one would be bail for him. But his attorney said he would get him through it, it was found that there was a flaw in the indictment therefore he is out again.

He took a house at the Back of the Retreat in the Harleyford row to make a passage through that way in case he should be called upon for money he slept there every night. The Landlord of that house knew nothing of him. He called for his Rent, but did not get it - he had taken that too for 28 years, and threatened to put a prostitute in there if he did not forgive him the rent, which he was forced to do, having other houses in that row. Uncle was forced to give him £30 to give up the Lease of the Retreat House.

For my services, 12 days, I am to have 3/6 a day, the Sale will be 20th of this month to be sold at Squills

Auction Rooms in the City, he being so full of business kept Uncle from putting up before. First, the Retreat was used as a School on the plan of Kings College, but that did not succeed. Barber thought a Billiard Room would answer but he was mistaken; no one coming near the place.

While I was there we had a leg of Pork for dinner. Mr Barber was not then arrested, there was a charewoman who was cleaning the house, his assistant, Harris, I and himself. Two days after Barber was arrested, & flung into prison. Well the Thursday morning when dinnertime came, he being arrested Tuesday, the woman went into the Larder for something for dinner, when lo the Pork was gone, where was it gone to! well we had bread & cheese, for Harris was gone out. When he came home we told him of the Pork, and he says the cat must have taken it[, it] could go no how else. I and the Woman wondered how the cat could run away with such a great piece. However, it was gone, I & the Woman knew that it went to prison to its master.

If I get my money I shall buy a New Hat, my old white one which I have been wearing this 3 years, ever since we came from Trowbridge, and some time when we were there, is very shabby & always made fun of in the street. There is a bad Hat! White Hat! and so on. I wear my Black one now which I had at the same place.

I have written our misfortunes, but perhaps I told you so before. However, through Mr Postans good nature we are more comfortable. Today Sunday 17th Charlotte came home from her place at Mrs Postans she has spoilt her hands working about, but thank God she will get the better of that now she is at home. We are in one of Mr Sadd's houses in the Retreat living rent free but for how long I d'ont know it is a great saving. Now Charlotte is at Home we must get some needlework for her to do. We buy two or three things one after another we have another old chair a fire shovel & Father will buy when he can a pail, mop, and other things

23

that we have not got, it goes on week after week and is never bought because we have a little debt or two to pay off first, but thank God We are able to do it. Uncle borrowed 5s off Father, so there is a change of circumstances, 2 months ago he would not look at us. Charlotte perhaps will live with them.

When we meet again, vous lirez donc l'histoire de nos malheurs. Wishing you health and Happiness and all the good things of this life, I Remain your affectionate Brother F Hale

Excuse the Shameful Writing

This Frederick died the next year, but his younger brother, Christopher Frederick must have decided he could do better overseas and left England. He was eventually caught up in the Californian Gold Rush which began in 1849 after the discovery of gold in the mountains of the Sierra Nevada in the previous year. On May 18th 1855 Frederick wrote to Alfred:

Salter Creek Amador County California   March 18th 1855

Dear Alfred

I recd your kind letter yesterday (the first during my residence in California) and hasten to reply to the same. I am very much grieved to learn the melancholy intelligence it contains. I was somewhat prepared to hear of poor Father's death on account of his age and infirmities - but I had no idea of my dear Sisters illness - much more death but Gods will be done - and let us hope they are happy in a better world. You say the last letter you recd from me was dated Aug 10/51 (I think you mistake) on account of yours coming to hand to the above direction which I sent you in a letter last November /54 - which I think you must have recd. I did not know as you surmised of your marriage - but I had an idea that it was your intention and now that you are so - allow me

24

to congratulate you on the happy event - wishing you all the blessings attendant on the married state. and I hope you will both live long to enjoy it - give my kind love to Maria and the nice little girl "Fanny" and her little dear brother "Alfred" (extract from the original) and I hope I shall have the pleasure of seeing them & all of you one of these days. I am happy to perceive by the tenor of yours and mothers letter that you have done all in your power to make our dear Mother happy my thanks especially are due to Maria for her kind attentions. God will bless you for the same. I am very sorry its not in my power to help you but I hope you will give me credit for the intent if you cannot for the deed. I hope as poor Fred used to say there "are better times coming".

I should think you are much more comfortable in Steeple Ashton than at the "Farm House" & I hope we shall have another game of Bagatelle there yet - As to myself I have very little to say I am still mining for gold with but indifferent success - the best "placer diggings" are mostly "worked out" and if I dont "strike it" I have done a pretty good show to stay here a few years longer - but never despair is the American motto and so we keep trying in the hopes of "hitting it". I hope you wont confound a California Miner with a Coal Miner said California Miner being a very different sort of an animal here we have Doctors - Clergymen, Merchants &c &c - all miners camping in a "Log Shantee". Thank God I enjoy excellent health and have never had a days sickness during my sojourn here -

Wishing you all the same believe me your
Affectionate brother Frederick Hale

P.S. I hope you will write again as soon as this comes to hand F.H.

He must have been out of touch with his relatives for a long time, for he apparently did not know that his father had died or that Alfred had been married for more than five years and now had two young children.

On the same sheet, Frederick wrote a letter to his mother, in which he was at pains to be reassuring:

March 18th 1855

My dear Mother

I recd your very kind letter for which please accept my best thanks, you my dear Mother have been sadly afflicted of late but I thank God he has given you health and strength to bear up against it. I am very happy to hear you say you are comfortable - and I shall always respect my brother and his wife for their kindness to you - as you say our family is now a very small one, but let us hope those who it has pleased God to call from us are happier where they are. I hope the little children will be a comfort and an amusement to you and hope you may live to see them grow up. I suppose you will recollect that my birth date comes in this month. I shall be 31 years old a pretty rugged fellow I can tell you allways out in the open air - up on the mountains this is a splendid climate & very little sickness. I have met two of my old Lima acquaintances here and one lives now within a quarter of a mile of me - which makes it very pleasant as one can talk over old scenes and old times in Town. I hope we shall be more fortunate with our letters for the future. Your letter was 5 weeks coming so we can hear from each other in 2 months by writing quick - which I hope you will do - and now my dear Mother accept my best wishes for your health and happiness and believe me

Your truly affectionate Son
Frederick Hale

When he wrote to her again on July 11th 1855, he was unable to sound so cheerful but was still anxious not to alarm her:

Salter Creek Amador County California   July 11 1855

My Dear Mother
      I recd your very kind letter dated May 14th which receives my best thanks. I am very glad to hear you are enjoying good health and hope you may be blessed with a continuance of the same.
      I did not think you were near sixty eight yet but I hope you will live many a year yet. I am sorry to hear all our old acquaintances are dying - but we all must bend to the will of God - much obliged for your kind remembrance of my birth day. Give my thanks to Alfred for his care and kindness to you. I always thought [he] was a perfect trump and I am very glad to hear you all live so happy together. I often wish I was with you for the quiet social life is not to be met with in California. I hope you enjoyed your trip into Kent but am very sorry to hear your sister is so badly afflicted. I hope my dear Mother you may be spared the same - I hope as well as you that I may be more successful and as you say it is not for want of application tomorrow I go into a new claim 3 miles from here and I hope I shall make something as I am "hard up" just now. I worked for a man last spring and he lost money by his claim and therefore I can not get paid but I think it is good and I shall get it some time or other. I hope you will continue to write on the recpt of each of my letters and I assure you I will not fail to do the same.
      It is a very great pleasure I can tell you to hear from our friends from the old country althought we get all the newspapers both American and European, French &c.
      Living is getting cheaper now in California a man can live now (cooking his own provisions) for $3 or 4 but the

Taverns charge $8 - When I first came to California I paid $15 per week for board and lodging. The Salter Creek is a Quartz mining district there are 5 water mills on the creek each mill having eight pestles or crushers some take out as high as $1,000 a week some $6 and 800 dollars. These mills are the main stay of the place - each mill employing about 20 men - water is the principle thing in the mines we have to pay 75 cts and a dollar an inch for it to wash the dirt with - to companies who construct canals on the tops of the hills - many of the hills having gold in them from the si...ct I hope you will excuse this short letter but I promise you a longer one next time - give my kind love to Alfred and his wife - and all the little "childer" and please accept the same my dear Mother

from your affectionate son   F. Hale

But by the summer of 1857 he had lost hope:

Stuart Flat Secret Ravine Placer County Cal:

Aug: 30 1857

Dear Alfred

I expect to reside on this flat for some months and therefore there will be no fear of your answer missing - I have not heard from you these 2 years - and I suppose I address the only remaining one of our family - I hope you will write as early as convenient on the recpt of this for although I have nothing of interest to tell you I shall be most happy to hear how you prosper in the world - as for myself I see nothing but hard work - near as bad as the labourer of England and I dont expect any thing better - I bought into a claim the other day for $160.00 paying $100.00 owe $60 yet - but am in hopes to make something in a few months - board here is $6.00 a week boots, clothing high, up to the present time I have had splendid health and have lost very little time or work - we work from 10 to 12 hours a day

Sunday excepted although on the Rivers they work longer and Sundays too - Robberies and Murders are very common here - I saw a gambler almost cut to pieces - he had about 11 stabs in him one cutting through heart and liver - this is getting to be what Americans call a "hard country" too much poverty - and too many that wont work - and too many that cant get it. Thermometer stands (110) hundred and ten in the shade and when you get ten feet below the surface of the ground to work I assure you its considerable better - there is a great deal of sickness this summer round here fever and ague principley. Since writing the above I understand the "Bear River Ditch" is giving out which will be a bad thing for me - but I shall have to stand it - as I have before Write for Gods sake for you are the only man on earth I can call friend

Yours truly

Frederick C Hale

He was thirty-three when he wrote this, perhaps his last letter, an exhausted, frustrated and desperately lonely man.

His brother Henry went to Australia. Though he was more successful than Frederick, he did not do so well as he had hoped. He wrote to Alfred on May 18th 1860 after several years of silence, during which he had been living, for at least part of the time, in Hobart, Tasmania. Now, however, his prospects were brighter:

Swan Reach Gipps Land Victoria   May 18th 1860

My dear Alfred
        If this Letter should find you out you will no doubt be suprised to hear from me after so long a time since I

29

wrote, I must begin by informing you I received all your Letters by the Steward of the Windermere and was very happy to hear you were all well as I hope you have been ever since. I was very sorry for poor Edwin his dying must have been a great blow to you all, and I am almost afraid to ask any thing about my Father or Mother but I sincerely hope they are both alive and well, I am glad to hear you are in such a situation and respected by Mr Long, his notice will bring the respect of the whole County on you.

I will now tell you the reason I have not wrote before. In the first place, I have not been Fortunate since I have been in these Colonys, I have had a living and something to wear and that is all. I know you would all of been glad to hear from me under any circumstances but as I had no good news to tell you I did not like to tell you bad to make you miserable.

I dont wish you to think I have been in want for I have not what I mean I have never rose any higher than when I arrived here, until now, I am happy to inform you I have been Fortunate at last in obtaining a situation as Overseer for Mr J Johnson, Member for Gipps Land, and am now living at Swan Reach his Cattle Station. I have about 3000 head of Cattle in my Charge for which he gives me £80 Year and finds Rations, and House to live in &c, and I expect he will rise my wages in time,

You informed me in your Letter that you were Married, to one of the Woods Daughters of the White Hart, I remember the House and the old Gentleman, but it is so long ago I quite forget Mrs A Hale. I hope you may live long and happy together, I have likewise got me a Partner and more than that 3 little Hales, 2 Boys & 1 girl, and as you say of your Wife a better I think could not be found, she is a Native of Hobart Town, her Sister a young Woman of 18 Years of age is living with us.

I left Hobart Town in consequence of things getting

in a very bad state there, and I am glad I made the change we are very comfortable here, we have all you require, plenty of Cows to milk & Horses to ride and a pleasure Boat for the Lake. The Station is on the Tambo River about 5 miles from Lake King, As regards what I have to do I have 2 men under me with whose assistance I look after the Cattle, it is all riding from one weeks end to another, and rather dangerous work sometimes as some of the Cattle are very Wild but not more than Fox Hunting in England all the difference is the Country here thickly Timbered.

Christopher [Frederick] seems to be leading a rambling sort of life like me he will get steady when he Marries, however I hope he is well, and doing well. Please remember me to my dear Sister and tell her me and my family are all well, and hope she is the same, tell her I am afraid I shall never see her again for if I come to England, I dont see how I am to live as I have no trade, and I am not much of a scholar, I should dearly like to see you all If ever I do I should have to come back here again, The expense of going to England & back would be about £60, but I am afraid Mrs H Hale would never consent to it, You must write to me about it, but if I cannot come if you will write I promise to Keep up a regular correspondence with you.

I am sending this Letter by a young man and his Wife friends of mine by the name of Mr Parker, they are just now starting for London, I shall direct to you at Mr Longs Road Ashton, but I shall tell them to call at the Poultry for information.

The station where I am living is 14 miles from the Main Road, so please direct for me, in the care of Mr Charles Marshall, Captain Cook Hotel, Nicholson River, Gipps Land, Victoria as that is the nearest House, the postman calling there twice a week. I must now conclude Give my Kind Love to my dear Father and Mother, and tell them the contents of this Letter, Give My Kind Love to Charlotte and Christopher and accept the same my dear Alfred from your Affectionate Brother

Henry Hale

By June 30 1877, however, he appears to have left the cattle ranch and be working as a contractor, probably in the timber business. This letter gives a vivid impression of the vast emptiness of the Autralian outback:

Cunninghams Lakes Entrance Gipps Lane Victoria   June 30 1877

My dear Brother Alfred

I recd your dated 16th Febr all safe and was glad to hear that you are still enjoying good health, I should have wrote before but I have been waiting to have my likeness taken, and sorry to say after travelling 120 miles and no railroad, the Artist had just left when I got there, I will certainly send you one on the first opportunity, you surprise me at the rate of wages now in England for I assure you there are hundreds of good men here working for 15s/ a week and plenty of ordinary men for 10/ a week, I have allways made it a rule as far as I could to work at contract work or as the Yankee would say on my own hook, and have hitherto done better that way, but still I have not been able to save anything, but thank God I am happy and comfortable and allways shall be as long as I have my health & strength. Tell my dear Neice Fanny to write to me as shall allways be glad to have a few lines from her, what a blessing it must be to you to have such a Daughter she indeed must be very clever, It must be a great boon to have such an Organ as you speak of is it in the old Church at Steeple Ashton I recollect the old place quite well, but it seems like a dream, I am glad to hear that your Son Alfred as so good a situation, As regards our railroad they have lately opened for traffic 40 miles of it and

32

expect 40 more to be complete by Christmas the whole distance from Sale. The starting point to Melbourne is 120 miles, the nearest terminus to me is 80 miles by water and as I have a good Boat I dont think much of going that distance in the summer time with a fair wind, it is a very pretty and pleasant place where I am living, the Lake is about 80 miles long and there are plenty of fish and wild fowl of every description, many a gentleman in England would give his thousands to have such a place to live at, speaking of my Trip to England, God knows that nothing would give me more pleasure than to come and see you, but I hope you will not think of it, excepting you can well affored such an outlay of money, I am happy to say that myself and Family are quite well, and we hope that you and yours may live to enjoy many happy years to come, and now dear Brother I must say good bye for this time hopeing to hear from you soon I Remain Your Affectionate Brother
Henry Hale

Six months later, his tone is more anxious; he seems more homesick, longing for letters and newspapers from England, in spite of the beauty of his surroundings:

Cunninghams Lake Entrance Gipps Land   Decr 15th 1877

My dear brother Alfred
I recd yours of Sep 17th all safe, and am glad to hear that you enjoy so good health. I likewise got the paper and a letter from my nephew Alfred which I was very pleased to get, he seems a very sensible young man and I hope he will do well. I am sending him a few lines this time, I expected one from Fanny tell her not to forget and I shall always be glad of a paper, I see by the paper that a person by the name of Wilkins is Keeping our old House the George Inn at Trowbridge, and that you are Quarter Master in the

Yeomanry. I am sorry to hear your Wife is so great a sufferer, but it is a great blessing to be where she can get the best of medical advice, I recollect the House Farmer Ball lived in when I was a boy and I think Farmer Tyler lived opposite at the corner going to the Church, let me Know I am correct after so long a time, it seems like a dream Since I wrote to you I have been Sawing Timber to build a church for the Aboriginal Mission Station at a place called Lake Tyers, but for the future I shall have to give up such laborious work as it is to much for me now. I must look about for a lighter job, since then I have been stripping Mimosa Bark, it as been bringing a very fair price until lately it is now very cheap in consequence of a deputation of Tanners waiting on the Minister and representing that if the export Trade was not stopped that Bark would Fail and they would have to be supplied from other colonies, they have now put a Tax of £3 per Ton on all Bark leaving the Colony, the people are very much dissatisfied about it, and well they may, as there is plenty of Bark everywhere, but they want it at their own price, Our Railroad will not be completed for 12 months, The weather here is very dry, and everything burnt up but we have had some bad Floods and very high winds, I did not get your letter in time to answer by last Mail this will leave on the 27th of this month, I must now wish you all a very merry a happy Christmas and with Gods blessing many of them, I am happy to say my Wife and Family including self are all quite well and hope this may find you the same, I must now wish you good bye my dear Alfred and Remain Your
   Affectionate brother
    Henry Hale (Send word how old you are)

In his last surviving letter, dated October 29 1878, he had moved into a small town where he was rather desperately seeking work. He was nearly fifty-six.

Henry's niece,
Fanny Hale,
later to marry
James Mottram
(See also p. 12)

Sale Gipps Land Victoria   Oct 29th 1878

My dear Brother Alfred
    You will surely think by this time, there is
something the matter with me, not having wrote for so long,
but thank God I am alive and well, I must now tell you the
reason I have been silent so long, I have shifted from the
Lakes Entrance since last March and from that time until now
I have not been settled anywhere, I am now living at Sale
and am still doing nothing, but I thought I had better write,
and send my likeness Knowing you would be glad to get it,
I am told it is a very good one, please send me one of yours
if you can, Tell my nephew Alfred that I shall not be among
the Mimosa Bark this season I have just returned from a trip
of 100 miles to look at some, but I could not find enought to
pay me, give my Kind Love to him and tell him I shall be
glad to hear from him at any time, Business is very dull
here everyone is complaining of the times, nothing doing, I

think things are worse here than in England, Monster Meetings of the unemployed are being held very often and the poor people are very bad off people are flocking here from Melbourne, now the Railroad is done, looking for employment at very low wages, this district being very small it is quite overrun, I have been living here nearly 3 months and have not as yet found anything to suit me, but live in hopes with the help of God to get something shortly, there is one thing provisions are much cheaper than they were, bread -/7d the 4lb loaf, Beef -/3d per lb Sugar -/3½ Tea 1/6 per lb Potatoes 7s/- cwt Butter -/7 per lb but the thing is to earn the money to pay for them, I pay about £25 per Year for a place to live in and no garden to it, You told me in one of your letters I was born in Decr 1822, so I must be 56 next Decr, I have 2 sons & 3 Daughters living, 1 Son and 2 Daughters at home, who are thank God with my dear Wife and self quite well, my eldest Son is married, I will send you my eldest daughter's likeness next time, I have nothing more to tell you this time, my dear Wife joins with me in sending Kind Love to you all, and that you may enjoy health and happiness dear Alfred is the wish of

Your
Affectionate Brother
Henry Hale

Address care of Mr H Hill Cabinet Maker McArthur St Sale Gipps Land Victoria

As they grew older, men in the colonies were apt to find themselves elbowed aside by new arrivals - younger, stronger, single men, more able to cope with rough living and heavy work and without dependents to support. But at least Henry was not isolated, as Frederick was, he had a wife and family and was in touch with his relatives in England. Nonetheless Alfred, who stayed at home, did better than these two brothers. When he died he was managing the estates of a country gentleman at Steeple Ashton, Wiltshire.

The millions of people who left Great Britain in the nineteenth century, seeking a better life elsewhere, came from every social class, from aristocrats to tramps. There were weavers, shop-keepers, ministers of religion like the Reverend William Bakewell who reluctantly resigned his post as minister at the Octagon Chapel on November 11th 1838 because, as he explained in this letter, he thought America offered better prospects for his children. He and his family settled in Pittsburgh, Pennsylvania.

Febry 12. 1839.

My dear Sir,

I have a persuasion that in my hurried & confused reply to your very gratifying remarks on the presentation of the very handsome gift from the Congregation, which I had not the most distant expectation of receiving, & by no means, did justice to my feelings, & I beg thro' you to express to my very generous friends my deep sense of this manifestation of their kindness, & their affectionate respect. As the time approaches of taking a final leave of so many valued friends from whom I have received many testimonials of their deep interest in my welfare, I feel more & more how great is the personal sacrifice which a sense of duty to my children has induced me to make, & tho' I am fully persuaded that in emigrating to America, I am doing the best for them, & therefore cannot repent my resignation of my ministerial charge amongst you, yet I feel how painful it will be to say farewell.

It is my earnest wish & prayer that you my dear friend & all the members of the Congregation, may experience in rich abundance the blessings of this life, & that the good hand of God may direct all your life, that you may be rich in the consolations & principles of religion & that hereafter we may be permitted thro' the mercy of our all gracious parent, to meet again in his heavenly kingdom.

Begging that you will express, as you may deem most proper, my sincere & grateful thanks & affectionate respect,

I remain very sincerely yours

W Bakewell

Perhaps the emigrants with the best chance of improving their conditions were the farm labourers. Thousands went from Norfolk. Provided they survived the terrible voyage in an emigrant ship without permanently damaging their health, they were sure of work in countries where huge tracts of land were being cultivated for the first time. They often took their families with them; if the parish was paying the fares, then the whole family had to go, from grandma to the youngest baby. The authorities were not going to be left with old people and infants to support. These men and women were used to hard work and harsh conditions. They usually found that food was more plentiful and cheaper and felt there was more chance of advancement and more freedom than at home. One Norfolk labourer wrote from the Australian outback 'Here everyone is as good as everyone else. Here there is no squire, no parson and no gamekeeper'.

Middleclass emigrants, like the Hale brothers, were in a different position. They usually went alone. Communications were slow and difficult; it was easy to lose touch with their relatives and friends at home. Their expectations, and those of their families, were often unrealistically high. Men like Frederick and Henry Hale, whose father had been a licensed victualler, had as boys been used to a comfortable home and a certain amount of culture. They were educated; they grew up in a world where there were books, newspapers, theatres, concerts and balls. In the colonies, or in rural America, they could find themselves living in a cultural and social desert and this grew more oppressive as they grew older.

Educated women who had moved to the colonies were even more likely to suffer from the lack of social and intellectual activity than the menfolk who had their work to interest and occupy them. Rosa Tanner, for instance, as a girl attended Surrey House School in Surrey Street, Norwich, a school where the education of girls was taken seriously. Here Rosa became very attached to Fanny Mottram, who had piano pupils in the school; and enthusiastically embraced Fanny's conception of the sort of life a well-educated woman could and should lead. So when Rosa went out to California to join her brother and his wife, she found life on his fruit farm intolerably boring and frustrating, as this letter shows.

Monday even^g 11 p.m.
Sept 3rd
1894

Box 93
San José
California
USA

My dear Mrs Mottram,

I have allowed almost 4 months to pass without thanking you for those sweet brave words of advice you sent me when I wrote and begged you to help me in my perplexity. They were just what I needed & made me quite determined that <u>some</u> change must be made in the silly trivial little lives we were leading. Scarcely a day has passed during these last months when I have not pondered over what you suggested, & I have read & re-read your letter untill almost know it by heart, for I was determined it should not be answered until we had made as you say "some steps towards retrieving our lives from emptiness".

I suggested the reading circle first of all, but the suggestion met with such very lukewarm support, for the circle could only consist of the three of us, for San José is 3 miles from here & there is absolutely no one, between this place & town, who has any ideas beyond apricots & prunes, at least no one that we know of.

Sometimes I feel sure that I shall grow into a prune myself, don't smile, it is really true! - & the little hard pebble of a stone which Dollie used to tell me took the place of my heart, is all ready to form the kernel!

Well, when cold water was thrown upon the reading scheme, I suggested that we might arrange to have really good music every Sunday even^g & so make a little distinction between this day & the other six. For our even^g some friends came in & we tried to spend the even^g so, but before it was over the good music degenerated to the silly sentimental & then to the comic songs etc & worse than all the utter failure of the even^g ended in a family quarrel. It was a bitter disappointment & I felt that I could not make another effort, for each attempt seemed to make matters worse. You are the only soul to whom I could tell all this, but somehow you seem to understand me in a way no one else does & pride does not prevent me from telling you of my disappointment, as it would if I were writing to another.

Please do not think I have been unhappy for this is not the case. Madge is a little darling & my life in the New World has so far been an exceedingly bright & happy one - liberty, society & plenty of excitement, to all out-ward appearances everything that could be desired - & prob^y if it had not been for the 2 yrs spent in Norwich & the influence of yours & the Surrey House friends lives & ways of thought, I should have been completely & entirely satisfied.

But I could not get away from the feeling that our lives were so completely "trivial" nothing to do but seek our own pleasures from Monday Morn^g until Satr night. Of course Madge & I have to help a little with the housework but this we can manage every day in about 1 hr. Ive tried to spend our morn^{gs} with needlework, then we had a gardening craze - but it did not last long & I felt a great yearning for work which would call into play more than just my physical strength.

In spite of Madge's opposition I sent my name into some Educational agents & last week had an offer of a post in a family - two children 9 & 11 with a salary of £70 resident. I could not have wished for anything better, but unfortunately the place (Yolo County) is about 2 days journey from here & Madge begged me not to go so far away. After having given up Surrey House to be with her, Yolo County was not much of a sacrifice. We had a long talk & many a talk together & she agreed that if I stayed here we would read and work together - that we would give up entertaining these so called 'friends' rather acquaintances who like us for convenience sake, that she should help me with music & that I should decide upon the books for our course of reading. I wrote & told Miss Katie how we had made out Time Tables & pinned them on our bedroom walls. We manage to work for from 7-8 hours a day, that is keeping the afternoons almost free. You cant think what a difference it makes, the days simply fly past. Jim scoffs at our latest craze, of course, but we have some books in the house now at any rate, which are worth read^g & tonight I saw him engrossed for quite a long time in "Sesame & Lilies".

This is the first change, the next is to be the giving up of the ranch - We have put it into the hands of an estate agent for an early sale, & just as soon as we can get a fairly good offer for it we are going to live in San Francisco - This, I know, will be a surprise - you are almost the first person I have told, in fact you are the first with the exception of Father & we only wrote to him last Sunday.

I know he will hate the idea of our giving up the house, & will almost insist upon our returning to England if we do so but we mean to stand firm.

I do not know what profession Jim will study for, he rather thinks of being an architect, but there is so much more opening for a boy here than in England, besides Madge says she c^d not live in England for a <u>month</u> after having been out here for so long.

I expect we shall all three have rooms together in

41

San Francisco, so that Madge can take lessons in sing^g & pianoforte, which she is very anxious to do & I will try & get a morn^g engagement, but it is almost certain to be a year before we can get rid of this place.

You will wonder what has made us decide to do this. We have been going into accounts lately & find each year the income is only about half of the expenditure & we cannot well reduce the latter. I hate to feel that Madge is drawing upon her capital in this way to keep up a place which has almost no attractions for any of us. Of course the last two seasons are supposed to be exceptionally bad ones, but then it is uncertain how many more exceptionally bad ones we are going to have - & then too I think this house is too large for the size of the orchards - & perhaps we are none of us very good managers - If Jim liked the life it would be different, but he has only just confessed to us, what we have for a long time suspected, that he cannot like the work, & indeed I do not blame him, for, for quite half of the year he has absolutely nothing to do & he is too young to spend so much time in idleness. We feel quite sure that we are acting wisely, & no home opposition shall make us change our plans.

Does Una ever write to any of my sisters? I know she asked me for an address once, in case she wanted to. If she does please ask her not to mention this, as we have kept it quite a secret until now.

What a delightful trip they must have had in Norway - I wonder whether you are at Overstrand as you were last year? It was sweet of you to remember my birthday & send me the loving message. Thank you so much for it. I am almost ashamed to send this letter after all, for I have just poured out all my thoughts & feelings, which, as Miss Katie complains, I always manage to hide with a laugh - always? but there are exceptions.

You will write when you can, I know, for your

letters are such a help, & the last four months have been a weary blank, while the future seems all brightness.

Do Ralph & Hugh remember me still, or have I passed quite out of their lives? Please give them my love - & the same to the girls, for this will reach you just when the term is beginning - Is Una wearing her brown cape this winter, & you and Miss Katie yours with the fur? I like to picture you all together, & would give just half my possessions to come back this time & lead the opposition in the dear old civil war that used to rage so furiously, that is if you would offer a shelter for the wounded at Bank House & heal up the wounds as you so well knew how to do.

Do you remember your blessing just before I sailed, the wish of the "Little Lord Fauntleroy" - "God keep you all the night, God bless you all the day - Rosa mine", the best and most embracing wish you c^d have sent, & one which at any rate, will never be forgotten.

Think of me sometimes & help me to be worthy of the love which you have given me - & to live a life you will not be ashamed of -

> With very much love from
> Yrs
> Rosa

['*Sesame and Lilies*' by John Ruskin, published 1865 and 1871, is a collection of essays on the respective duties of men and women, as Ruskin saw them.

'Una' was Unity Mace, one of Fanny Mottram's closest friends. She came to Norwich in 1878 with Maria Clarke, who started the Surrey Street school, where Fanny taught music and her sons Ralph and Hugh began their schooling. 'Miss Katie' was Maria's sister, Catherine, who taught at the school.]

Some of the most attractive material in this collection concerns the upbringing and education of children. There are, for instance, two letters from Maria Clarissa Wood, Fanny Mottram's mother, aged thirteen and at boarding school, to her mother.

Somerford 29th May 1837

My dear Mother,
     So short has the time appeared since I have been at school, that I can scarcely believe I am again about to join my beloved friends at home, but still I trust that quickly as the time has passed you will find by the improvement which I have made, that I have endeavoured to be attentive, as I am now of an age to value your kindness, in allowing me so many opportunities for gaining that knowledge which may hereafter render me a useful member of society.
     Miss Williams requests me to present her best respects, and inform you that our Summer Vacation will commence on Wednesday, the fourteenth of June.
     With kind remembrances to all dear relatives and with duty to my dear Father, and yourself, believe me my dear Mother
        Your affectionate daughter
        Maria Wood

Somerford   November 27th 1837

My dear Mother,
     I am very sorry indeed to hear that you are not recovered from your illness. I hope you will be well enough to come to the ball which will be on the 7th of December. Miss Williams desires me to present her respects and she will be glad to see you or any of the family. The performance of our little drama will commence about six oclock in the

evening. I look forward with pleasure to the holidays when I shall be able to spend a short time with you. I hope you will find me much improved in all my studies. I have endeavoured to pay attention and to learn as much as the time would permit. Miss Williams likes my frock very much indeed she thinks it very pretty and neat my dear Mother I do not know how to thank you for it but I will repay your kindness in some when I go home. Please to remember to all friends and believe me to remain

Your dutiful and affectionate daughter

Maria Wood

It is unlikely that any thirteen year old today would address a parent so ceremoniously. Relations between parents and children were then much more formal and distant. It is more than likely that the letter was inspired, if not actually dictated, by the mistress. The school, at Somerford, Wiltshire, would be in a private house, where a small number of girls would be instructed in the deportment and accomplishments thought suitable for young ladies. They would be expected to do various kinds of fancywork and produce objects suitable for presents, or for ornamenting the home, such as the bookmark in the collection, which has the words 'Inscribed Thine for ever' worked in cross stitch on paper, mounted on pink ribbon.

James Mottram, Ralph's father, did not go away to school. He was educated at home by governesses until he was eleven. His was a small family by the standards of the time - just two boys and a girl - so until he went to school his contacts with children of his own age may have been somewhat limited. Fortunately, however, when he was still quite young, he began to go for long holidays to stay with relations. This was instructive; he experienced life in places as different as an Essex farm and the city of Liverpool, then one of the greatest ports in the world. Even more important, these visits brought him into contact with a host of cousins - his uncle Rankin, the Essex farmer, had four sons and seven daughters. In such homes, where James was immediately acceptable because he was a relative, he could have easy relationships with boys and girls of all ages. Cousins were the only girls with whom a boy like James could associate on friendly terms. It is not, therefore, surprising that in families like his, there were so many marriages of cousins; James' first wife, Charlotte Rolfe, was his second cousin. The marriage of relatives was especially common amongst Nonconformists like the Mottrams. Their choice was limited because they were expected to choose partners of their own religious persuasion. Marriages of first cousins were disapproved of, though they happened, but marriages of second and third cousins were commonplace. This led to vast, immensely complicated networks of relatives, as among the Quaker Gurneys.

Some of the boys that James met on these holidays became close friends and corresponded with him. His cousin, J. H. Johnson from Overstrand, wrote about a treat which proved more alarming than enjoyable. After he had been taken to see a travelling menagerie at Cromer, he wrote 'I have been to see some wild beasts and it made my stomach ache to hear the lions roaring. The rhinoceros was very ugly and looked dirty. I gave the elephant only one apple because I was afraid at first'. Another cousin, Charles Cooper from Liverpool, was obviously out to impress eight year old James.

> Liverpool
> Jan 26 1843

My dear James,

I am much obliged to you for your kind letter, and I am glad to say my eyes are very much better. There is a young gentleman's school at Heswall and when we were there they used to come up and carry me on their backs and take me to fish and sail a beautiful boat which one of them made for me it is a foot and a half long. You asked me if I had read any of Peter Parley's Tales I have read six of them and like Earth, Air, and Sea, the best. I have read the Swiss family Robinson and like it very much. When I was at Heswall I had a couple of Rabbits they were very pretty but when we came to town I was obliged to sell them. You will be sorry to hear that our Beautiful big blag dog Nep is dead we have had his skin made into a rug. I have been reading a nice book called Extracts from Travellers illustrating Scripture. Give my Love to uncle aunt and cousins

        Believe me

        Yours affectionately

           Charles T. O. Cooper

[The first Peter Parley books, published in the USA in 1827, were written by the American Samuel Goodrich. The pseudonym 'Peter Parley' was later used by several English writers of instructive books for children.]

With his second letter, Charles sent a drawing of his boat, carefully coloured in crayon. James' cousin, William Rankin, was almost a big brother to him. When William heard that James was to go to school he wrote reassuringly about the fun he and his schoolfriends had had on Guy Fawkes night.

Totteridge   Dec 8th 1845

My dear James,

        I have to thank you for a letter I received from you a short time since and I would have answered it sooner if I was not so much engaged in preparing for the examinations which are taking place every day however as I am at leisure this evening it is with great pleasure I give you a few lines in return. I was sorry to hear you had been suffering from rumatism I hope you have by this time recovered You would have liked to have seen the fun we had here on the 5th of November. A gentleman who lives near invited us all to go and take tea at his house and in the evening to let off fire works and have a bonfire in his park. We went to the number of forty and spent a very pleasant time of it there was 5£ of fireworks besides plenty of squibs and crackers for us to throw about. This morning as we were just going into school Mr Thorowgood sent for our class into the dining room we were all expecting a good talking for something we had done but instead of that he said as it was a fine morning he thought we should have no objection for a walk. So we went out with one of the masters while the rest stayed in school. We have had some snow and good hard frosts lately and I was in hopes that we should get some skating before the holidays but last night there was a heavy storm of rain which thawed all the ice. I hope you will like the school you are going to and be as happy as I have been at this. And now my dear James with love to Uncle Aunt and Cousins

      Believe me
      Your affectionate Cousin,
      William Rankin

There were, however, no plans to send James to boarding school. Instead he joined a small group of boys taught by John Withers Dowson in his own house in Norwich. Dowson, an active member of the Octagon congregation, was a dedicated teacher who encouraged his pupils to have wide interests. There survive some of the essays which James contributed to the school magazine on topics as varied as 'Ancient Britons' (with some spelling mistakes corrected), 'Railways' and 'A Visit to Liverpool'. In another essay he described a visit to the remains of the Roman town of Caistor-by-Norwich, a school trip, perhaps. James had been there before and had picked up bits of Roman pottery.

By the time he was fifteen and a half, James had finished with schooling and, on March 19 1850 he entered Gurney's Bank (where his father was manager) as a clerk. His grandmother wrote to congratulate him.

Hambridge   June 15 - 50

My dear James,

I am sorry to hear you had a troublesome cough but trust from the accounts we have had you are getting rid of so unpleasant a companion. I will write a line to show you, you are not forgotten by me, I shall enclose in this note a half sovereign which I beg your acceptance of, and although you are become a man of business which I am delighted to hear you are happy in I think you will not object to this small trifle from your affectionate Grandmama

Mary Mottram

Ralph Hale Mottram, the writer, was born in October 1883, the eldest son of James and his second wife, Fanny Hale. Ralph's younger brother, Hugh, was born on January 29 1886. Their parents, like all careful parents of the business and professional classes, then and previously, believed that basic education, especially for boys, should begin in the home and as soon as possible. Relatives encouraged little boys to read by sending them letters printed in capitals. Hugh did not need any encouragement to write. Alice Minns, one of the maids, who was looking after 'Baby' (then two) while his mother was away, wrote to her:

Bank House   Norwich. Sept 12th 188- [1888?]

Dear Madam,

Just a few lines to say how Baby is. I am afraid I shall find it rather hard work to write in his Compny he wants to help me, I have given him paper and pencil he says he is writing to Mother - - - -

I just left this letter a second and he told me he had made a boat - - - Baby is so happy & full of fun as usual he says send me love to Mother and two kisses and now he is saying not so many.

I have said all now with love & kisses from Baby,
I remain yours
  Obedly
   A. Minns

Children were taught to write by an older person guiding their hand. A letter from Ralph to his half-sister Helen dated April 5 1888 has a note in his mother's hand, 'Mother held my hand but I really moved the pen all by myself and Mother let me do RALPH all alone'. He was then four and a half. Another letter of his ends abruptly 'I am getting tired of Alice holding my hand. Goodbye.'

Religious instruction began early. Alice took Hugh to chapel with her when he was not quite three and later reported to his mother:

       Bank House
       Norwich
       Sept 9th 88.

Dear Madam
You will be glad to hear how Baby is & what he is doing etc he is very good & happy, ... this morning Baby went to Chappel with me he was so good he only spoke once about some little boy comeing in, I never saw a child behave better ... he was pleased when I told him, he was to have a boat when Mother comes home, he says Mother gone to London to see Queen - - -

Hugh's good behaviour was a tribute to Alice's management; he was a very active boy and chapel services in the 1880s were not designed for the entertainment of the very young. Alice was not a nanny nor even, officially, a nursemaid; the boys had a nurse when they were babies but were always brought up in the family, never isolated in a nursery. Alice was literate, she wrote a legible hand and expressed herself clearly, though with the occasional spelling mistake. She was devoted to Hugh and he to her; his mother could and did go away, knowing the boy would be lovingly cared for with plenty of fresh air and long walks in Norwich. 'On Monday we could not go out in the Morning it was so wet' she wrote, 'in the afternoon we went down to the Ferry. Tuesday was a lovely day in the morning we went for a little walk & then into the Castle Gardens in the afternoon we went up Thorpe Road, today we went to the Rosary this afternoon the Castle gardens Baby likes going there he likes climbing the steps ...'

Although education began early, there was plenty of time to play and toys to play with. We have a glimpse of Hugh, aged fifteen months, 'on the floor of the breakfast room enjoying the drum' and of five-year-old Ralph sitting on the windowsill holding the boat he had made - sails of paper, ropes of black wool, flags of ribbon. On January 3 1889 Ralph wrote to his half sister Helen, 'I have had a Christmas tree it was lit up it simply looked lovely. Father Christmas brought me a Bugle and a lovely box of soldiers called Black Watch' [letter in Norwich High School archives].

By this date most people had trees and gave presents at Christmas. Earlier, February 14th, St Valentine's Day, had been the time for present-giving. In Norfolk this custom continued, as to a certain extent it still does. The account books of Ralph's father James show him buying Valentine presents every year; in 1851 these included 'collars for the servants 3/10d'.

It is indeed fortunate that these papers have been preserved to give us vivid and authentic glimpses of everyday life in the past. Ralph Mottram used this collection as material for his life of his father James, 'Portrait of an Unknown Victorian' written in 1936, and in his volumes of reminiscences. There remains much of value to the social historian that could be extracted from this collection, which includes many papers of later date than those quoted here.

The earliest of the letters quoted here was written in the 1730s, when George II was King, the latest is dated 1899, in the vastly different world of late Victorian England, more than a century and a half later. During this long period of rapid and far-reaching social change, family life itself had altered. The attitude to marriage had become more romantic, women had become more independent, parents less remote from their children though still far from indulgent. Millions of English people had gone to live and work overseas, often losing touch with their relatives at home for years, or for ever. Because more men than women emigrated, the balance of the sexes in the home population was altered and more English women remained unmarried than had been the case in the earlier periods. All these changes are reflected in these papers, which have so fortunately been preserved for us to enjoy and learn from.